My Voice
To
The Lord

The Reverend John A. Shalhoub

My Voice
To
The Lord

The Reverend John A. Shalhoub

ISBN 1-55630-515-X

PUBLISHED FOR
REV. JOHN A. SHALHOUB
727 BARN STREET
JACKSONVILLE, NORTH CAROLINA 28540

PUBLISHED BY:
BRENTWOOD CHRISTIAN PRESS
4000 BEALLWOOD AVENUE
COLUMBUS, GEORGIA 31904

Dedication

To
my boys:

George,
Michael,
Samuel;

my wife:

Awatif;

and

my mother:

Nour

Foreword

I see the inspiration and the blessing of God in these pages. John makes writing a primary way to work through and solve problems.

We were both outsiders because our family and cultural roots were far from the coastal Carolina community where we've settled. As outsiders we experienced some lack of acceptance and accommodation. In my case, less so because with my English ancestry and surname I blended physically and was soon able to talk like a native. With John's Lebanese ancestry and accented speech people will never assume that maybe he's from around here any more than people might mistake me for a native of Beirut. John has experienced, more than many of us, the pain of unfairness and discrimination. The question he raises is not so much about unfair treatment, but rather, response to those who see you only as a stranger in their midst.

The contemporary problems and joys of mankind find their way into John's writing. As he presents and wrestles with them, these situations become our own. He constructs responses, which invite and enable us to feel God's connections to our own lives. His writing opens this perspective to us in surprising ways. He chooses everyday words and phrases that are easily understood on an everyday level. The surprises come when he introduces a twist or change in perspective that sparks higher level understanding of everyday experience.

When faced with adversity in relationships, I tend to struggle and bog myself down with the friction between myself and others. John, more wisely, accepts that this condition exists for all people and then struggles to find the words and phrases needed to express those feelings as an essential part of ours.

The Psalms endure because the writer was able to express God's connection in the everyday concerns of his people. As a United States Navy chaplain, family counselor, and school counselor, people with every imaginable situation seek John's help.

Dale E. Weston

Contents

Preface

John's writing connects directly from his heart to my heart. Through his writing I more clearly understand my own experience, both my sorrows and my joys. I find comfort in discovering that I am not alone with my thoughts and feelings. John shows me the connections to God in my everyday life.

About a dozen years ago, we met as new teachers at the same high school. John's assignment was to work with the students who got in trouble. He required his students to write about their problems and how to solve them. In time the walls of his classroom were covered with proverbs which the students had written. And John practices what he teaches. His poetic and prayerful advice published in the Saturday paper both awakens and comforts us. When I happened to mention his column in a night school class, many students said that they read his prayers and even cut them out and save them. May you, too, find a special meaning in his words.

Our friendship deepened as I learned more about John's love of God and his love of writing. He joyfully uses his gifts from God as he writes. With honesty he shares his feelings and with courage, his faith. With powerful simplicity he describes what it means to be fully human, and to be fully loved by God. May the verses in this book become blessings for you and bring you closer to God.

Dale E. Weston

Introduction

"Prayer is the test of everything."

My Voice To The Lord is more than teaching us how to pray, it teaches us that through prayer we experience God's power in our lives. Since we came to existence, God has empowered us to communicate with Him. Through prayer we thank God for His blessings, we thank Him for our families and friends; we thank Him for our lives; and we thank Him for His guidance and support as we struggle through tragedies, disappointments and failures in our daily lives.

Our Lord Jesus Christ taught us to pray and to communicate with Him through prayer. He said, *"But thou, when prayest, enter into thy closet, and when thou hast shut thy door, pray to thy Father which is in secret; and thy Father which seeth in secret shall reward thee openly"* (Matthew 6:6), KJV.

So everyday we pray for all those we love and all those for whom we care. Prayer brings us into unity with one another across land, water and space. Prayer brings us into the presence of God as He listens to us when we call on Him for help.

Let me say this, *Just as the birds need wings to fly and roam the skies freely, so people need prayer to carry them without hindrance to God's love.* Only through prayers and perseverance can we overcome the trials and the tribulations of everyday. Father John, in his prayers, offers prayers that encourage us to face up to the hardships of life and to the challenges of the vanity of arrogance with courage and perseverance. His prayers also prepare us to confront the unpredictable challenges of time.

11

Furthermore, he offers us the splendor and the glory of God through a unique poetic and biblical style that matches the Psalms with beauty, elegance, and, spiritual uplift. *He brings us into union with God through the love of our Lord, Jesus Christ and the communion of the life-giving Holy Spirit.* He always knocks on God's doors to ask Him to soothe our hurts, to lift us up from our pain, and to heal our wounds.

Father John always stands for fairness, compassion and integrity. He is just like John the Baptist who cried in the wilderness to prepare the way of the Lord. He seeks refuge in God's infinite forgiveness and love.

He feels that the more we pray, the more we are assured of God's presence in our lives. We need to grow and mature in faith in the knowledge of God through prayers that bring us forgiveness, healing, and comfort. The Lord talked to us about the importance of prayer. He said, *"Therefore I say unto you, what things soever ye desire, when ye pray, believe that ye receive them, and ye shall have them" (Mark 11: 24), KJV.* And that is what Father John does everyday in his prayer; he invokes God's love and compassion for our sakes and the sake of those he loves.

> *Centuries ago, St. Theophan attested to the importance of prayer, "Prayer is the test of everything; prayer is the source of everything; prayer is the driving force of everything; prayer is the director of everything. If prayer is right, everything is right. For prayer will not allow anything to go wrong."*

Father Dr. George Shalhoub
Associate Professor of Religion/Philosophy
Madonna University, Livonia, Michigan

Come To Me

Come to me, O my people;
follow me.
Fear not the cruelty of this world.
I am just, fair and kind.

Let me carry your burdens.
Walk with me.
The journey is too long,
and your feet are weary.

Come to me, O my people.
I am your friend;
talk to me.
I am listening to you.

I'll hear your cries
when you're hungry,
and I'll wipe your tears
when you're in pain.

Seek my ways.
Obey my commandments,
and you'll find refuge,
safety and comfort.

I will not allow despair
to wreck your heart
nor fear to destroy your faith.

I am the light of the world,
the Beginning and the End.

I will deliver you from your pain
and grant you eternal life.

Just come to me,
my people!

"Child, Did You Pray Today?"

My mom said,
"Child, did you pray
for your good health today?"
I answered,
"Mom, what for?
I already have good health."

My mom said,
"Child, did you pray for your job
today?"
I answered,
"Mom, what for?
I am safe and secure in my job."

My mom said,
"Child, did you pray for your brother
and sister today?"
I said,
"Mom, what for?
They can pray for themselves."

My mom said,
"Child, did you pray
for your neighbor today?"
I answered,
"Mom, what for?
They are not my concern."

My mom said,
"Child, did you pray
for common sense?"
I answered,
"Mom, would you please leave me alone,
I don't need to pray."

One day I lost my job.
I became sick.
I became angry with God
for allowing all these things
to happen to me!

One morning my mom walked
into my room and said,
"What are you going to do now?"

I looked at her and said,
"Mom, don't you see?
Now I am praying!
I am praying for a lot of things."

16

Evening Prayer

The day has come to an end.
I thank You, Lord,
for your allowing me to make it
through the day.

Grant me a comfortable
and peaceful night
that I may live another day.

I ask that this evening,
and this night will pass by
without any problem.

Lord, my God,
forgive me
if I sinned this day,
whether by word,
deed or thought.
You are good
and loving toward mankind.

Lord!
Grant me peace and hope
for You are my God,
Protector and Savior.

Deliver me
from all the temptations
of the evil one.

Raise me up again
in proper time
that I may glorify You.

You are blessed,
now and forever,
Amen.

Before I Go To Sleep

O Lord, my God,
into Your hands I entrust
my soul and body
for safekeeping
and protection.

Surround me
with Your holy angels
whether I am asleep or awake.

Shield me from the assaults
of my enemies --
the visible and invisible.

Sanctify my soul.
Safeguard my body.
Correct my ways.
Cleanse my mind.
Deliver me from the trials and
the tribulations of this world.

In Your name, Lord Jesus, I pray,
Amen.

Morning Prayer

Thank You, O Lord,
for giving me this day.

Good morning and
glory be to You.
Blessed be Your name.

I pray that You are not angry
with me.

Please don't hold me
accountable
for my foolish mistakes
nor for my bad judgment.

Please discipline me
and correct my ways,
but don't deliver me to death.

Help me to improve my attitude.
Give me good health,
a good mind,
and the will to do my work well.
Please be with me always.

Assign Your holy angels
to protect me and my family
and all those who
love to serve You.

In Your name, Lord Jesus, I pray,
Amen.

My Petitions To The Lord

I pray for all the people
who are present here, our families
and friends, that the Lord
may grant us all good health,
sound minds,
and protection from evil.

Lord, hear my prayer!

I pray for (*this place*),
and all the people everywhere,
that they may live in the peace
of the Lord.

Lord, hear my prayer!

I pray for the President of this country
and for our armed forces everywhere,
that the Lord may aid them
to preserve peace and harmony
among all the peoples everywhere.

Lord, hear my prayer!

I pray for peace and prosperity
all over the world,
and the union of all mankind.

Lord, hear my prayer!

I pray for good weather,
abundance
of the fruits of the earth,
and for peaceful times.

Lord, hear my prayer!

I pray for travelers by sea, land,
and air, and for their salvation.

Lord, hear my prayer!

I pray for the sick,
and the suffering
and for their recovery.

Lord, hear my prayer!

I pray for the deliverance
of the captives,
and the oppressed
that the Lord may help them
to live productive lives.

Lord, hear my prayer!

I pray for our deliverance
from affliction, danger
and hunger.

Lord, hear my prayer!

I pray for peaceful and natural
death without pain and suffering,
and for the salvation of our souls.

Lord, hear my prayer!

Minister To Us, O Lord

Lord, I don't have the will
nor know the way.
I pray that you will give me the courage,
and the knowledge to navigate
in a difficult world.

Help me to avoid the pitfalls
of my life's journey.

Allow me to be in control of my life.
There are too many people
over me who share my life with me.

Teach me to be as gentle, attentive,
and helpful to others
as I want them to be to me.

Broaden my mind to be thoughtful,
understanding and supportive
of the people who are around me.

Assist me to help people
to learn new skills,
improve performance and be happy.
Permit me to be a good role model
to the people I work with,
and to the people who work for me.

Guide me to give others sound directions.
Humble my pride to follow the directions
of the people who have authority over me.

My goal is to promote harmony,
achieve success
and complete God's mission.

We are living in a world of technology,
and we are in need of more education and learning
to bring humanity
out of ignorance and poverty.

Let us be the instruments of knowledge
and the guiding posts of hope
to all generations.

Fill our hearts with love,
clear our minds from confusion,
and facilitate our ways
to know the truth,
to be fair and tolerant of others.

Help us to provide comfort and support
to the forgotten and the oppressed.
Awaken our senses to combat evil,
hatred and bigotry.

Transform our hearts into vessels of love,
compassion and mercy.

Save us from ourselves when we are unable
to recognize the truth.

Alert us to be aware of one another's needs.

Whenever we gather together in Your name,
help us to plan, organize
and coordinate the activities
that will make our ministry a mission
of love and fellowship.

Ministry is our mission,
kindness is our way
and service is our goal.

Let Your light shine before us
that we may truly be called
the children of light.

The harvest is ready
and the workers are few.

Every minute of our life is very precious.
So let every effort be genuine and fruitful
that we may wear the crown of victory.

Yesterday, today and tomorrow,
Your message is the same.

Let us remember Your mission
in our lives.

In Your name, Lord Jesus, I pray,
Amen.

My Personal Prayer

O Lord, my God!
Enlighten my mind.
Forgive my sins.
Heal my infirmities.
Grant me peace.

O Lord, my God!
Bless and protect my family,
relatives, and friends
who are loyal and committed to You.

Remember them with kindness and love.

Remember with favor
family members and friends
who departed this life.

Protect the Church from violence.
Make it grow and prosper
to carry on with Your mission
in the world.

In Your name, Lord Jesus, I pray,
Amen.

I Pray For My Family

O Lord, my God!
Grant our families understanding,
wisdom and love.

Prosper their ways,
heal their infirmities,
forgive their sins.

Touch their hearts
with kindness, comfort and joy.

Safeguard them from harm,
shield them from the evil forces,
and protect them from the attacks
of all enemies.

We pray that You will hear
their petitions
when they call on You for help
whenever there is a need.

Broaden their minds,
fill their hearts with happiness,
and blanket them with Your love.
Bless their going out
and their coming in.

Bestow on them good health,
sound mind and grace,
that they may always praise
Your holy name.

In Your name, Lord Jesus, I pray,
Amen.

May God Revive Your Hope

May our God revive your hope
just as the soft rain revives
the thirsty land.

May the Lord answer
your prayer,
and guide your way.

May He give you
assurance of peace
to live another day.

May He give you
a sound mind to know the way.

May He grant you good health
and safe travel
as you journey through
this world.

In Jesus' name I pray,
Amen.

It Is A New Day

It is a new day --
New hope, vision and life.
O Lord!
Renew our hope, vision and life.

It is a new day!
Grant us a desire, flexibility
and ability to live as a happy family
according to Your commandments.

It is a new day!
Tame our anger with kindness
and compassion.

Curb the human violence
with Your heavenly guidance
and fatherly authority
that we may live in peace.

It is a new day!
Broaden our minds to seek wisdom.
Touch our hearts to receive grace
and to give love with humility
and kindness.

It is a new day!
Uproot oppression with fairness
and kindness.
Replace our bigotry with tolerance
and understanding.

It is a new day!
Uplift our spirits to accept
what we can't change.
Energize our spirits
that we may work in situations
that demand patience and sacrifice.

It is a new day!
Let it be a new day every day!
Let it be a day of trust, mercy and caring
that we may serve one another's needs
with acceptance and friendship.

It is a new day!
Banish want, fear,
and despair from among us.
Cast away wars,
poverty and suffering.

It is a new day!
Let it be a day of the family,
education and spiritual renewal.

It is a new day!
Upgrade us for the glory of Your
holy name,
and for the peace of the world.

In Your name, Lord Jesus, I pray,
Amen.

Today

Today I am free of anxiety
and worry.
I am happy, relaxed
and cheerful.

Today I am kind, gentle
and generous.
I am courteous, friendly
and charming.

Today I am genuine,
truthful and happy.
I am tolerant, compromising
and forgiving.

Today I am free of stress,
anger and moaning.
I am strong, resourceful
and patient.

Today I set aside the worries
of the world,
and overflow with faith,
hope and charity.

Today I am sociable,
friendly and helpful.
I am in the world
with a laughter and a smile.

Today the Lord lives in me.
He gives me peace,
and sets me free.

Today I live for tomorrow,
and tomorrow is for today.
I want to know you,
and you to know me.

Come today, join me,
tomorrow is today,
and today is tomorrow.
Let us make the best of today.

Life is you and me;
we need to work together
for a better world.
Today is Today!

Teach Me, O Lord

Teach me to be respectful
to those who work with me and listen
to those who talk to me.

Help me to learn a skill
to provide for my family and
all those who are dependent on me.

Teach me
to accept people the way they are,
whether they are rich or poor.

Show me how to be trusting,
understanding and believing
in people I know
and people I don't know.

Open my ears to hear
the moaning of the oppressed
and the sighs of the neglected.

Provide me with compassion and love,
and assist me
to help those who need my help.

Teach me to appreciate
success and to accept the bruises
of defeat.

Allow me to hear Your voice
in my inner heart and to cope
with the hustles and bustles
of humanity.

Let me hear Your voice
in the sadness of heart
and in the despair
of my spirit.

Permit me to hear Your voice
with the wind
and in the silence of night.

Make me mindful
of the needs of others.

In Your name, Lord Jesus, I pray,
Amen.

May His Peace Be Our Peace

May His *compassion* save us
from the hardships of the day
and may His grace console
our broken-spirits.

May His love *heal* our wounds
and His wisdom enlighten our minds
that we may become disciples of
forgiveness and hope.

May His *love* shower us
with kindness and friendliness
that we may become His instrument
of mercy and peace.

May His *truth* guide us every day
to face our daily tasks with a heart
full of inner strength and energy
that we may accomplish them
with a heart full of thanks to Him.

In Your name, Lord Jesus, I pray,
Amen.

The Lord Saves The Day

When the world turns against you,
and it seems
that there is nowhere else to go,
in that very moment,
the Lord steps in to save the day.

He hands you an invitation
to His dinner table
and points out the way
to His mansion.
He hands you a map
and a compass,
and the rest is up to you
whether you want to go to the banquet.

Cruelty has increased in the world
and multiplied;
and many people are hurting
each other without provocation
or cause.
O Lord, our world is hanging in space;
and therefore,

we are in need of You
to keep it in balance.

Please help us to keep away
sickness, misery and pain.

The people who choose the wind
will reap the storm,
and those who choose evil,
will reap evil.

But those, who accept God,
will know His love
and forgiveness.

God's love sustains the people
who love and care for one another.
His mercy will touch their hearts
and comfort their souls.

The souls of the just
and the righteous
will harvest the blessings
of kindness and the joy of peace,
but the wicked will not rest.

The eternal God will never
slumber nor fall asleep.

His faithful children
will not fall nor stumble,
for He is always there for them.

He keeps them safe
and secure under His wings
forever and evermore.

Amen!

Lord, Answer My Prayer!

My God who is in heaven!
Grant me vision, strength and skills
to be an effective combatant against
evil, illness and violence.
Sustain me to maintain peace,
kindness and goodwill.

Open my eyes to understand
the meaning of life
as I knock on Your doors
in search of answers
to questions about what
is in store for me in this world.

Revive my faith,
awaken my senses,
and guide me
to know the way
in this difficult world.

You are my heavenly Father,
and I am Your child.

The bond between You
and me is forever.

I know in my heart that
You are always with me.

Please allow me to be always
with You.

In Your name, Lord Jesus, I pray,
Amen!

Help Me With My Decision

My God, Your way is the way
and my way should be according
to Your way.

Whatever I want and do,
let it be according to Your will,
O my God!

Allow me to be loyal to You,
today and every day.

O Lord, my God!
I am stressed and confused.
Grant me a sound mind
and keen judgment
to make the right decision.

Please let my decision
be the right decision
that I may not have
to worry myself to death.

In Your name, Lord Jesus, I pray,
Amen.

The Lord Is There For Me

I said to my self,
"Why should I pray today?
No one would listen to me anyway."
But I prayed anyway
expecting nothing in return,
and the Lord heard me
and blessed me.

I said to my self,
"I'll make no more decisions,
because there is nothing going my way,"
but I made them anyway,
and they were the right decisions.

I said to my self,
"The future looks grim and dreary,
and I fear darkness and failure."
But I did what I could anyway,
and the Lord rewarded me
for my courage.

I said to my self,
"The world is in upheaval,
and it appears that the end is near.
So why should I work anymore?"
But I worked anyway,
and my work was greatly appreciated.

I said to my self,
"Why should I give my time to people?
There is no one who would appreciate
my services."
But I continued to serve them anyway,
and I was grateful
when they were there for me.

I said to my self,
"I wish I could get rid of degradation
and humiliation."
The Lord answered me,
"I shall restore you
with honor, grace and integrity."

I said to my self,
"Even if I want to live in peace,
there is always someone
who would bother me."
But I continued to be kind
and friendly to everybody,
and the Lord enriched my life
immensely with His love.

I wished on the stars;
I prayed for the rain to fall.
I thanked my loving God
who always listened to me.

And now I realize that
the Lord is always there
for me.

May The Lord Bless Us

May the Lord our God enlighten
our hearts and minds.

May the comfort of the Holy Spirit
touch our lives
with love and compassion.

May the Lord our God forgive our sins
and enrich our days
that we may live in peace.

May the Lord of all creation
and the Master of our destiny
grant us sound minds, kind spirits
and warm hearts to live peacefully
throughout our journey in this world.

May the Lord our God increase
the production of our labor,
and protect our health
with the healing power of the Holy Spirit.

In Jesus' name I pray,
Amen.

Touch Us With Your Love

With Your love,
touch our hearts.

With Your mercy,
forgive our sins.

With Your wisdom,
correct our ways.

With Your compassion,
overlook our shortcomings.

With Your grace,
bless our souls.

With Your power,
protect us from evil.

With Your bounty,
nourish our bodies.

Grant us sound minds
and honest hearts.
Sustain us with love and hope.

Protect our families.
Bless their going out
and their coming in.

Bring understanding
and peace to our world.

Broaden our minds
to know the truth.

Keep us strong, free
and loyal to You,
our families
and our nation.

Fulfill our legitimate dreams
and awaken our hopes.

Guide us to serve humanity
with fairness and compassion.

Embrace us with Your love
and affection.

Uplift our spirits in time of crisis,
stress, and pain.

Brighten our lives with hope,
courage and success.

Reside in our hearts
and never leave us
without support.

Allow Your holy angels
to ever guard us
against disasters,
sickness and oppression.

In Your name, Lord Jesus, I pray,
Amen.

Bless This House, O Lord!

O Lord, our God, bless this house,
its foundation and the land
on which it stands.

Bless all those who dwell in it.

Sanctify them by the power
of Your Holy Spirit,
and through the love of our
Lord, Jesus Christ.

Forbid Satan, his angels
and their agents from entering
this house, or any of the people
who live in it,
and those who associate with them.

Make the residents of this house
shrines for Your holy presence.

May they receive Your blessing
and protection,
for You are a compassionate,
merciful, and forgiving God.

Heal them from every malady
and grant them Your peace.

Arm them with the truth;
fill them with love
to live pious and honorable lives.

Guard them with Your holy angels,
day and night.

Shield them from harm
and from the influence of the devil,
his agents and all the wicked spirits.

O Lord, our God!
Empower your servants
with the power of Your holy Cross.

Arm them with spiritual strength
and supply them with wisdom
that they may overcome despair
and conquer evil.
Surround them
with Your holy angels,
and support them with the prayers
of the saints.

Protect them from danger
all the days of their lives.

All in Your name, Lord Jesus,
Amen.

Your Will Be Done

Lord our God, today
and every day,
we pray that Your will be done
in our lives and in our world.

Have mercy on us.
Cleanse our minds from
evil thoughts.

Purify our souls from sin.
Heal our infirmities.
Protect us from evil
and grant us peace.

In Your name, Lord Jesus, we pray,
Amen.

Save Us

May the Lord save us
with His grace.
May He give us strength
and sustain us with hope.

May He protect our lives from harm,
and guard our souls from evil.

May He guide us
to go about
doing our daily work
with dedication and loyalty.

May He grant us
His peace that we may always
live in peace.

All in Jesus' name,
Amen.

May He Show You The Way

May the Lord show you
His way that you may know
the way.

May He answer your
prayer as you pray
for good health
and daily bread.

May He give you
the compassion
and the wisdom you need
to be genuine,
kind and loving.

May His love
and peace prevail
in your daily work
every day.

May He be with you whenever
you reach a dead end.

In Jesus' name I pray,
Amen.

Go In Peace

As you march into the world,
keep your hearts and minds
on the Lord.

He is your shield
and armor.

He is your Redeemer
and Savior.

He is your hope
and peace.

He will arm you with insight,
wisdom and skills.

He will shower you with His
blessings forever
and evermore.

You may go in peace.

The Lord Still Loves Us

The Lord still loves us
despite our hatred,
greed and ignorance.

The Lord still loves us
despite our cruelty,
deception and vanity.

The Lord still loves us
despite our impatience,
cynicism and indifference.

The Lord still loves us
despite our tyranny,
oppression and anger.

The Lord still loves us
even when we fail to feed
the hungry, clothe the naked,
and free the captives.

The Lord still loves us
even when we refuse to soothe
the pain of one another,
and wipe the tears of the hurt
and the forgotten.

If it were not for God's love,
the world would have been
condemned to eternal darkness.

The Lord still loves us,
in spite of ourselves.

Lord, Bless My Work

Almighty God and Lord!
You are my refuge and support.
You are the fountain
of wisdom and compassion.

Guide me; broaden my mind
to accomplish my tasks
with pride and satisfaction.

Grant me the vision to be creative,
industrious,
and faithful to my work.

Be my guiding light
and caring counselor when
things don't go well for me.

Help me to learn
in order to improve
my performance,
and to be faithful to the people
with whom I work.

Let me be kind to the people
who work for me.

In Your name, Lord Jesus, I pray,
Amen.

When In Trouble

O Lord, my God!
You are my help and support.
Be kind and gentle to me.

Please hear my prayers
and have mercy on me.

Deliver me from this trouble
that I may live a peaceful life.

I believe that trials and tribulations
will provide me with the challenge
to know myself better,
to deal with my problems
more skillfully,
and, most importantly,
to know that You are always
with me.

Bring me back to You
when I am adrift and disobedient
to Your commandments.

Please deal with me
not according to my sins,
but according
to Your compassion and love.

I am Your child.
Grant me Your divine grace
and arm me with patience
that I may overcome the hardship
and the anguish of my adversity.

You know my problem, pain,
and need.
Be my hope and refuge.

I am fleeing
to You for relief from my
helplessness.

Save me;
I trust in Your fatherly love
and forgiveness.

Please deliver me
from this worry.

Turn my stress and sadness
into comfort and joy.
Help me that I may praise
Your holy name always.

In Your name, Lord Jesus, I pray,
Amen.

I Am In Trouble

Trouble, trouble,
O Lord, I am in trouble.
Trouble is within me
And trouble is around me.

Help me O my Lord;
help me to overcome my troubles.

My life has turned upside down.
I am surrounded with thorns
of the flesh all day long.
My enemies have enjoyed
setting traps for me,
but they fell into the snares
of their evil thoughts.

Lord, I am tarnished from within
and without.
My friends have turned against me,
and I am drowning in my own tears.

But You, my Lord, have given me
refuge and hope.
I sleep with the pain of my heart
and I wake up
with the anguish of my soul.

I look to Your *Mountain*
where I find refuge
and to Your *Lighthouse*
where I find hope.
You have touched me
with Your love,
and healed me
with Your forgiveness.

Lord, extend Your hands and lift me up
Whenever I fall into the pitfalls
of my foolishness,
and into the darkness of my soul.
I have become like a lamb that
is led to the slaughter.

My tears have washed my face
and my fears blurred my vision,
but You, O my Lord, will cleanse me
from sin with Your love and forgiveness.
You will make me as white as snow.

You have forgiven my sins
and restored my soul.
O my Lord,
allow me to wake up in the morning
to praise Your holy name,
and to tell about Your good deeds
in the assemblies of the ungodly.
For *You are my Lord,*
God and Savior.

You Have Saved Me!

I humbly thank You
for Your loving care
and tender mercy.

You have heard my
prayers.
You have graciously
delivered me
from my troubles.

Please continue to bless me
with Your grace that I may
continue to follow Your
commandments.

Guide me to live a healthy,
peaceful and virtuous life.

In Your name, Lord Jesus, I pray,
Amen.

Bless Our Labor

I am on the way to work,
O my Lord.
Bless me this day and every day.
I thank You today
and every day.

Allow me
to share with You the light of day
and the quietness of night.

Keep danger away from me,
protect me from harm
and sanctify my soul.

Grant me this day to understand
the people who I work with,
and to respond to the needs of those
who work for me and with me.

Provide me
with the spirit of willingness
to respond to the needs
of my fellow workers
as well as of other people.

I pray that my work will be
for the glory of Your holy name,
and for the edification of Your people
who are fulfilling Your mission.

Work is sacred.
Bless the work of my hands
and the fruits of my labor.
Let me appreciate the work of others
and the contributions they make.

Let me appreciate life,
and the rewards of my work.

May this day be a day of gratification,
satisfaction and fulfillment.

May Your love provide support
to those who have difficulty in relating,
interacting and communicating
with one another.

I pray that we may accept each other
without any judgment or criticism.
Blessed are those who work
to add joy to our lives.

In Your name, Lord Jesus, I pray,
Amen.

Prayer During Travel

O Lord, our God!
Be my companion, guardian
and guide during my travel.

Protect me from all dangers.

Safeguard me with Your divine
power
that I may be safe from trouble,
and from unexpected difficulty.

I place my trust and hope
in You.

Be kind and merciful to me
that I may ascribe glory
and praise to You --
Father, Son and Holy Spirit.

Amen.

Flying Prayer

We are airborne above the clouds,
marveling at Your creation.

As we look out the windows
and hear the plane's engines,
we become assured
that we are safe and secure
in Your hands.

We feel Your love
as we focus our attention
on You,
because
we are under Your protection.

Your concern for our welfare
enriches us
with courage
and self-confidence.

O Lord, our God!
Calm our fears, mollify our anxiety,
and keep us safe.
Your spirit, O Lord, assures
us that we are shielded
from danger.

Allow us to reach our destination
that we may be with our families
and friends.

Blessed are You for protecting us!
Blessed is Your Holy Spirit Who gives us live.
Blessed is our Lord Jesus Christ
Who provides us
with assurance and inner peace.

In Your name, Lord Jesus, I pray,
Amen.

Guide Me, O Lord

Lord, give me the energy
to live another day
and faith to keep evil away.

Grant me insight
to follow the light in the morning,
in the evening and at night.

Protect me and my family
from hard trials and tribulations.

Provide me with knowledge
to combat sickness,
poverty and injustice
in order to live in peace.

Help me with all that I ask for,
for the good of us all.

Guide me to guide others
to avoid trouble and bad times.
In Your name, Lord Jesus, I pray, Amen.

Lord, Forgive Me

O Lord, my God!

I worship and glorify You
at all times in heaven and on earth.

You are patient with my foolishness
and compassionate with my needs.

I am a sinner.
I bow before You
and ask for forgiveness.

I am sorry for my sins.
I beseech You to be with me.
Show me the way
that I may not get into trouble again.

Direct my life to do Your will.
Sanctify my soul,
purify my heart,
and cleanse my thoughts.

Lead me not into temptation,
but deliver me from evil.
Encompass me with Your
holy angels.
Shield me from harm.
Guide me by the power of Your
Holy Spirit.

Engulf me with Your love
that I may always feel Your warmth
and kindness.

Allow me to know You
and to thank You for all You have
done for me.

You are my God.
I owe You my appreciation
and thanks.

In Your name, Lord Jesus, I pray,
Amen.

Help Me To See The Truth

Who knows the inner heart,
but You, O Lord?

Who knows the truth,
but You, O my God?

You have lifted me up
from the bottom of the pit
and saved my soul
from the attacks of my enemies.

You have opened my eyes to Your truth
for the truth of men is marred by deceit
and hypocrisy.

O my God!

I have cried to You for fairness
and begged for Your mercy,
because the world refused
to accept the simple truth.

Forgive the people
who have pursued cunning,
and treachery against me.
Show them the right way.

O my God!
Ease the pain of my soul.

Soften the throbbing stings
of my anxiety.

Your way is the way,
and the way of men
is pride and vainglory.

Save me from the intrigues
of the vicious cycles in this world.

Deliver me from evil.
Protect me from corruption
and temptation.

In Your name, Lord Jesus, I pray,
Amen.

He Is Your Armor And Shield

As you march into the world,
keep your hearts and minds
on the Lord,
for He is always with you.

He is your guardian and guide.

He is your armor and shield.

He is your vision and hope.

He arms you with knowledge
and skills.

He showers you with love and mercy.

May His blessings always
be with you.

In Jesus' name I pray,
Amen.

General Meeting Prayer

O Lord, our God!
Thank You for the opportunity
that brought us together
to explore ways
to serve those who believe
in Your mission.

We ask you, O Lord to ...

Give us wisdom to make
the right decisions.

Grant us courage
to carry out our duties.

Provide us with vision, patience,
and skills to solve our problems.

Broaden our minds and fill our hearts
with love to care for one another.

Give us wisdom and humility
to respect all the people.

Educate us to understand
one another
without being judgmental
or critical of our differences.

Supply us with the proper means,
and resources to serve
those who are in need of our services,
whether in sadness or in joy.

In Your name, Lord Jesus, I pray,
Amen.

Ecumenical Prayer

O Lord, our God, we belong
to different religious backgrounds
and teachings,
yet we are united in our goals
to worship You.

We are united to uphold moral,
spiritual and social values
that will strengthen the
societal fiber of our world.

We pray that we may respect
each other's
rituals and practices.
We pray
that we may promote fellowship,
preach tolerance,
and encourage cooperation.

Our objective today
is to facilitate the worship
of the Almighty God,
who cares for all of us.
Our faith groups are like boats
floating in the ocean.
There is room for each one.

Each one of these groups
is ready and willing
to help the other groups
in order to maintain
a stable and peaceful society.

Christianity is that ocean
in which all
religions, denominations
and sects are afloat.

O Lord, our God,
Your church is diversified
in views and theologies,
but we are working
together as a team
for the glory of Your holy name,
and the salvation of mankind.

In Your name, Lord Jesus, I pray,
Amen.

Lord, Honor Us With Your Presence!

O Lord, our God!
Honor us with your presence
today and every day.
Guide us to place You
in our hearts.

Provide us with the spirit
of fellowship, congeniality
and friendship; to be honest,
cordial and ambitious.

Make us instruments
of Your peace in this world,
for by doing so,
we will be glorifying
Your holy name in the world.

In Your name, Lord Jesus, I pray,
Amen.

Prayer Before Meal

From the fruits of the land
and from the water of the deep,
satisfy our needs from Your
bounty, O Lord.

*****

Bless us, O Lord,
and bless the food and the drink
which we are about to receive
from Your bounty,
for You are holy and blessed,
Amen.

Prayer After Meal

Thank You
for the fruits of the land
that sustain our bodies
and for Your grace that
nourishes our souls.

Thank You for the food
and the drink
which we have received
from Your bounty,
for You are holy
and blessed,
Amen.

O Lord, Fulfill Our Needs

O Lord, our God,
direct us to do Your will.
We beseech You to be with us
that we may know what to do
in order to live peaceful lives.

Grant us the desire to listen
in order to understand one another
with patience and tolerance.

Help us in this confusing world
to be loving, kind and helpful.

Protect us from evil.
Be our Shepherd and Savior.

You are our God and to You
we lift up glory and honor,
now and forever,
Amen.

Meeting Prayer

Thank You, O Lord,
for guiding us
towards
the achievement of our goals
in this meeting.

Thank You
for giving us this opportunity
to appreciate Your blessings.

Thank You for Your heavenly
and earthly gifts which we
have received
from Your bounty.

Thank You for Your love
and compassion for mankind.

You are a good God
and unto You we lift up glory
and honor forever and ever.

Amen.

May Your Life Be Fulfilled

May your life
blossom like a rose,
and your dreams like flowers.

May your hopes
be filled with optimism,
and your goals
be achieved with glory.

May your road be always
smooth and friendly.

May your star always shine
over you.

May the Lord
be ever on your side
and His love flourish in your heart.

May His peace
always be with You,
and His grace bring
you kindness and joy.

I Need Your Care, O Lord

Lord, my God!
I am only clay.
Please shape me according
to Your way in love,
wisdom and humility.

What I am
and what I can be
is Your gift to me.

I call on You day and night,
please hear my prayer.

You are my Lord,
Redeemer and Savior.

Please don't forsake me;
I am in need of You.

My heart is searching for You.
My mind is exploring ways
to learn more about You.

My soul is longing for You
that I may have peace.

Instill in my heart the will to care
for my own and others.

Teach me to learn new ways
in order to do my daily tasks
and activities more efficiently.

Help me to help myself and others.
Provide me with kindness,
that I may be kind
to those who walk through my doors
to seek comfort and support.

Ease my frustrations,
calm my emotions,
and teach me patience.

Awaken my senses to avoid hurting
anyone in my life.

Guide me to be compassionate
to those whom I came to know
and with whom I work.
Teach me to accept
and understand others
the way they are and the way
they appear to be.

You know my weaknesses
and you know my foolishness.
Don't allow me to be the victim
of my weakness nor of my foolishness.

Please save me from confusion
and protect me
from the evil forces of the universe.

In Your name, Lord Jesus, I pray,
Amen.

Hear My Plea, O Lord!

My God, You are the architect
of our lives,
the designer of our souls,
the builder of our bodies,
and the master organizer of our world.

We lift our hopes and dreams
unto You when justice fails
and corruption prevails.

Touch our hearts;
awaken our senses;
broaden our minds that
we may know the truth.

We beg You with our tears to help us.
Heal our wounds.
Soothe our pain.
Correct our ways.
Spare us from the insensitive cruelty
of our foolishness.

My God!
Teach us to be merciful,
loving and forgiving.
Enlighten our minds and hearts
that we may understand
Your purpose in our lives.

May Your hands guide us through
the maze of our ignorance
and may Your love save us
from the eccentricity of our selfishness.

May Your light steer us away
from our prejudices and biases
that we may become caring, giving
and forgiving in order to live in peace.

In Your name, Lord Jesus, we pray,
Amen.

Lift Me Up, O My Lord!

O Lord!
I am praying to You
at this difficult time of my life
as I bring my needs to You.

Hold my life in Your hands
and give me hope.
I am very sick.
I am in pain.
I am suffering.
I need Your tender mercy.

Guide the physicians,
and the nurses to help me in the process
of diagnosis, treatment and recovery.

Give me strength.
Let Your will be done and not mine.

I feel helpless and childlike.
Give me comfort and support.
I need to cope with the pain,
and to recover from my ailment.
Soothe my pain and save my soul.

My body is weak.
Please uplift my spirit.

Touch my heart
with Your love and kindness.

I know that we are here for a little while,
and that You will call me when it is time
for me to be with You.

You are the Keeper of my life,
Savior and Redeemer.

Please allow the rest of my life
to be peaceful,
without pain or struggle.

Heal my soul and body.
Forgive my sins that I may glorify
Your holy name all the days of my life.

O my Lord!

Permit me to draw energy
from Your loving kindness.

Don't forsake me nor condemn
the weakness of my heart.
Don't allow me to fall into the hands
of cruel and cynical people.

You are the One I need.
I am dedicating my life to You.

Please don't punish me
for my offenses,
but discipline me
to be holy and faithful to You.

Preserve me from harm
with Your love.
Heal me with Your compassion
and forgiveness

O my Lord!

Protect me from the assaults
of the evil forces.

Let me see joy after despair,
life after death
and dignity after humiliation.

Guard me
with Your holy angels.

Guide me with Your shining light
in this world,
and that which is to come.

In Your name, Lord Jesus, I pray,
Amen.

Relieve Me From Pain!

O Lord, my God,
I lift up my prayers to You,
hear me when I call on You
from the depth of my heart.

Relieve me from my pain.
I beg You to have mercy on me.

Restore my confidence in myself
that I may sing songs of joy
and dance the dance of victory.

I lift my pleas up to You,
hear my voice.
Give me Your peace, O my Savior,
and hold me in Your arms
that I may feel the comfort of Your love.

I raise my thoughts to You,
and I ask for Your compassion
and forgiveness.
Embrace me with Your love,
and allow me to thank You
for Your tender mercy.

Open the doors of Your kindness,
O my Lord,
and grant me the right
to receive Your loving care.

In Your name, Lord Jesus,
I pray, Amen.

Protect Us, O Lord!

Lord, our God!
Hear our prayers.

Answer our requests.
We need You; help us.

We have too many problems.
We don't know what to do!

We seek Your support and guidance.

Bring us into Your loving care
and protection.

Be our guardian
and protector whether at home,
work or wherever we may be.

Guide us to know
what is right in Your sight.

Draw us nearer to You that
we may live virtuous
and peaceful lives.
Allow us
to live under the protection
of Your holy angels.
Guide us to do Your will that
we may always praise
Your holy name.

Grant us wisdom to be kind,
charitable and industrious.

Bless our work, families, and homes.
Grant us good health
and help us to learn new skills.

Shield us from the assaults
of the evil forces of this world.

Supply us with energy and
the ability to resist temptation.

Arm us with strength to avoid
the corruption of humanity.
Redeem our souls.
Heal our bodies.

Safeguard our hearts
from harm.

Seal us with the Seal
of your Holy Spirit.

Grant us forgiveness,
reconciliation and salvation.

In your name, Lord Jesus, we pray,
Amen.

When I Am Sick

Lord, have mercy!

O Lord, my God,
Who heals souls
and bodies.

Visit me!
Heal me with the power
of Your Holy Spirit.

Restore me to full health
that I may praise Your
holy name forever and ever.

If I have any transgressions,
grant me forgiveness of sins
whether by thought, word or deed.

Bless me that I may live in Your grace
for the rest of my life.

In Your name, Lord Jesus, I pray,
Amen.

Heal Me, O Lord!

You are the healer
of my soul and body,
O my Lord!
Lend Your ears
to my requests.

Hear my voice
whenever I cry to You for help,
and whenever I am in stress,
in anger, or in pain.

When I call on You,
Please come to my assistance.

Listen to my smothered heart.
Wipe away my tears.

Raise me up from my bed
that I may thank You for healing
me from my sickness.

Whenever I am in pain and
the medicine is not helpful,
and the physicians
are unable to help me,
You, O Lord, can heal
my whole being
with the touch
of Your Holy Spirit.

You alone can give me the courage
to face up to my health problems.

I need You when I can't face up
to my pain and suffering.

The body is frail, the spirit is weak,
and the mind is confused and tired.

Protect me from evil and from all
those who seek to harm my soul.

To whom will I turn
when my life is beyond control?

To whom will I turn to
when my life is in despair?

You, O my God, the life, the health
and the healing of my soul
and body.

Grant me healing,
forgiveness and peace
that I may always praise
Your holy name.

In Your name, Lord Jesus, I pray,
Amen!

Lord, Give Me Strength!

Lord! Help me;
I need You; please help me.
My days are getting shorter,
my heart weaker,
and my sight dimmer;
please help me.
I need You; please help me.

Lord! Don't allow me
to be a burden on anyone.
Give me strength to move around
without falling.
I need You; please help me.

My tears are flooding my heart.
My fears are paralyzing my mind.
I beseech You to give me strength
that I may praise Your holy name.
I need You; please help me.

Lord! Grant me peace.
Please drive fear away from me.
Assure me of Your loving care.

Please help me to know You,
and to understand
how I fit in Your world.
I need You; please help me.

Lord! I pray that You may help me.
Please don't leave me nor forsake me.
I beg of You to uplift my spirit.
I need You; please help me.

Please come into my heart.
Please come in.

I feel empty.
When I gaze at You on the Holy Cross,
I feel crushed with pain and anguish.
I need You; please help me.

Give me strength to call on You for help.
Give me strength to share Your victory.
As I pray to You, please give me hope.
Don't leave me nor forget me,
I am Your child.
I need You, please help me.

Please, answer my prayer.
Hold my hand.
Energize my heart.
Make me an instrument
of Your love and peace.

I need You; I need You.

Who Touched Me?

"Who touched Me,"
The Lord asked?
I did O Lord,
why do You ask me who touched You?
You know that *I need You.*

"Who touched Me," The Lord asked?
I did, O Lord, You know all about
my pain and suffering.

"Who touched Me," the Lord asked?
I did, O Lord, You know all about
my problems, trials and tribulations.

"Who touched Me," the Lord asked?
I did, O Lord, You know all about
my sins, weaknesses and frailties.

"Who touched Me," the Lord asked?
I did, O Lord, You know all about
my doubts, frustrations and setbacks.

"Who touched Me," the Lord asked?
I did, O Lord, You know all about
my fears, hesitation and indecision.

"Who touched Me" the Lord asked?
I did, O Lord, You knew all about
me before I was born.
Why do You keep asking me
who touched You?
My faith is weak, my soul is weary,
and I am as helpless as a child.

Lord, have pity on me.
Take me by the hand and lift me up.
The Lord felt my pain
and had pity on me.

He said,
"Child, I am glad
'you have touched Me.'
I am not *testing* nor *judging* you.
Just call my name,
and I will be always there for you
'to touch you'
with My love and care."

Walk With Me

Walk with me,
O my Lord.
Walk with me
when my heart bleeds
and when my feet get tired.

Walk with me.
Walk with me when my tears
flood my eyes
and when I cry to You for help.

Walk with me.
Walk with me
when I can't reach the moon
and the stars,
and when I don't know
my directions in this world.

Walk with me.
Walk with me
when I can't endure my pain
and suffering,
and when I can't cope
with the problems of my life.

Walk with me.
Walk with me
when my family deserts me,
and when I am alone
and no one else wants to talk to me.

Walk with me.
Walk with me when I become
a stranger in my own home,
and when I have no one else to share
my joys and sorrows.

Walk with me.
Walk with me
when I don't understand my life
and when my neighbors put me down.

Walk with me.
Walk with me like a father walks
with his child,
please, just walk with me.

The Lord admonished me
with this words,
"Child, I am always *walking with you,*
keep holding onto My hand,
*I won't let you down
nor will I turn My back
against you"*

Prayer Before Birth

O Lord, our God!
You are lifegiver,
loving, and kind.

You have fashioned man
and woman from the earth,
and breathed into them
the breath of life.

You granted them Your
blessings that they may
increase and multiply
through the birth-giving
of children.

I ask You, O Lord,
to bless me and my child.

Provide me with comfort
and support
at this difficult time.

Make my labor an easy one.
Help me to deliver my child
without any complication.

O my God!
I thank You
for Your compassion.

Bless me and my child.

I pray that the child,
who is being born of me,
will bring me joy
and fulfillment
for the rest of my life.

In Your name, Lord Jesus, I pray,
Amen.

After Birth Prayer

Let us pray!

O Lord Jesus Christ,
You were born
from the Virgin Mary for our sake.
Give me Your blessings
for the healing
of my soul and body.

May Your Holy Spirit
dwell in my child and me.

Surround us both
with Your holy angels.

Guard us from evil,
protect us from every jealous eye,
and have mercy on us
according to Your great mercy.

Protect my child from every harm,
and from the snare
of every adversary.
O Lord, our God,
bestow upon my child
Your heavenly benediction,
that he/she may come to know
and adore You in Your holy places.

For all glory, honor
and praise are Yours,
now and forever,
Amen.

Stand By Me, O My Lord!

Lord Jesus be my friend.
Loneliness is so deadly
and dreadful.
I am scared and terrified
and I have no friend.
Please be my friend.

Hold my hand,
lift me up and speak
to my heart.

Listen to my thoughts.
Comfort my heart
that I may cope with stress.

There is no one else
to soothe my pain.
I am helpless
and broken down.

Spark a new hope in me,
and uplift my spirit.

There is no one else
to cheer me up.

Restore my hope
in a peaceful life.

Be my support.
Please stand by me.

Please release me
from my trouble
and set me free.

Guide my ship into
your port of safety
where I find refuge
and protection.

Enlighten my soul
to understand myself
and others that I may become
a better person.

Broaden my mind
that I may become creative
and industrious.
Allow me to be a model
of faith and decency.

O Lord, my God,
hear my prayer.
I appeal to You with
the tears of the afflicted
and the cries of the depressed.

Bring this world into harmony
of mind and heart
in order to live in peace.

Spare me from the terror
of the day
and the dangers of the night.

Hear me when I call on You.
You are my friend,
guide, and hope.

In Your name, Lord Jesus, I pray,
Amen.

I Trust You, O My Lord!

I trust You, O my Lord,
to uplift my spirit with confidence
and to bestow on me Your blessings.
I trust You to enter my heart
and to breathe life into my body.

I trust You, O my Lord,
to empower me with Your love
and to arm me with Your compassion.
I trust You to transform my weakness
into strength and my fear into bravery.

I trust You, O my Lord,
to energize my soul with Your Holy Spirit
and to heal my body with Your care.
I trust You to spare me from pain
and suffering,
and to restore my broken spirit
with Your loving care.

I trust You, O my Lord,
to hold my hand and to walk
with me across the road.
I trust You to walk with me to the Cross,
and to share with me Your victory.

I trust You, O my Lord,
to carry my burdens and to forgive my sins.
I trust You to keep evil away from me,
and to shield me from harmful spirits.

I trust You, O my Lord,
to give me a peaceful mind
and to grant me a clear vision.
I trust you to stand by me
when I am in trouble,
and to keep me upright
when I lack judgment.

I trust You, O my Lord,
to travel with me
that I may I reach my destiny,
and to show me
the beauty of Your creation along way.

I trust You, O my Lord,
to reside in my heart
and to heal my body and soul
forever and evermore.

When Depressed

O Lord, my God!
When I am in despair,
depressed and saddened,
I ask for Your comfort and support
to find pleasure in things
I care for and love to do.

I am in need of hope and courage
to continue living my life.
I am unable to enjoy what I do,
nor have I a will to go on living.

I am alone and lonely.
Turn my weakness into strength
that I may take pleasure from doing
what I desire and want.

I am in need of You to be with me.
Please don't allow me to give up
the rein of my life.

Save me from my pain and anguish.
I feel as if it is the end.
I am in need of a new start.
I want to feel good
about my life again.

I am grateful for Your blessings.
Help me to be in control
of my thoughts and actions.

I need Your help to do what I can
to be fully in charge of my life.

All I want and need is to be free
from anguish, pain and anxiety.

Help me to know You better,
and to know myself well.

I want to be full of laughter and smiles.

I want to sing again and be full of cheer.

Grant me faith, hope and the will
to accept myself as I am.

In Your name, Lord Jesus, I pray,
Amen.

Quell My Fear

O Lord, my God,
as You stilled the raging waves
of the sea,
I ask You to still the raging
torrents of my fears.

Calm the violent rages of my anxiety.
Replace my confusion with
assurance and certainty.

Reside in my heart;
nourish my soul;
grant me genuine faith.

I am traumatized with fear,
overwhelmed with pressure,
and thrown off balance
with indecision.

I am hopeless,
helpless and aimless.
My inner emptiness is grinding
my whole being.
I feel so worthless.

Come into my life,
O my Lord.
Give my life some meaning
and direction.

In Your name, Lord Jesus, I pray, Amen.

Deliver Me From Temptation

O Lord, my God,
hear my prayer.
I am in trouble.
Help me!

Please hear me
when I call on You.
Listen to the voice
of my supplication.

Direct me
to follow your precepts
from now on.
Broaden my mind
to recognize the truth.

Open my eyes.
Hold my hand just like
a father holds his child's
hand that he may not fall.

Allow me to understand
who I am,
and where I am going.

Here I am;
deliver me from my trouble.
I am lonely and depressed.

Give me hope.
Uplift my spirit that I may know
that You are with me.

Teach me patience.
Arm me with love and tolerance.

Forgive my offenses
which I have committed,
whether knowingly
or unknowingly.

Teach me
to rise above difficulties.

Show me the way.
Grant me joy and peace.

Be a loving father
and a big brother.
Wipe away my tears.
Soothe my pain.
Lead me not into temptation.

Allow me to praise and glorify
Your holy name.

In Your name, Lord Jesus, I pray,
Amen.

Deliver Me From Bad Habits

O Lord, my God!
Save me from bad habits.

Deliver me from temptations.
Spare me from guilt
if I offended you and myself.

My flesh is weak;
my impulsive desires
are very strong.

I don't have the willpower
to fight back.

Please surround me
with Your holy angels.

Shield me from the temptations
of the flesh.

I am caught in the cobweb of evil.
Help me! Heal me!

I am helpless
and without direction.

I have become a slave
to my impulses and desires.

I am deceived by the glamour
of good times.

Keep me away from drugs,
alcohol and compulsive gambling
and their bad influence.

Grant me the courage and the will
to suppress my urges and desires
that I may live a healthy life.

O Lord, my God!

The temptations are too many
in my life.

Many of them are harmful
to myself and others.

Deliver me from the grip
of their dangerous consequences.

Dwell in my heart.
Provide me with support,
guidance and wisdom in order
to control
my behavior and be well again.

In Your name, Lord Jesus, I pray,
Amen.

Calm My Angry Soul

O Lord, when I am angry,
I become like a beast,
and, when I am frustrated,
I fail to be rational and thoughtful.

I say words that are offensive
to You
and hurting to others.
By the time I realize that
what I did was wrong,
it becomes a little difficult
to apologize for my rude
attitude and unseemly behavior.

My hope is that
You will forgive me.
Without Your forgiveness
I am a dead soul.

Please, O my Lord,
calm the rage of my angry
soul with your kindness and love.

I am empty, unhappy,
and ashamed of myself.
I feel angry, obnoxious and ugly.

Help me to change my perception
of myself:
thoughts, feelings and deeds.

Be there for me when I lose
control over my life.
I no longer have
a clear vision of my future,
nor am I able to think clearly.

When I am unable to be in control
of my life,
I want You to take over my life,
and be in control of my destiny
that I may reach the fulfillment
of my life.

The only consolation I have
now is that You are willing to
forgive me,
and that You are willing to set me on
the right path that I may learn
to be patient,
thoughtful and considerate
of the needs of others.

In Your name, Lord Jesus, I pray,
Amen.

Rise O My Soul

I am a recovering alcoholic,
O my soul.
My name is Joe.

I take my time, one day at a time,
moment by moment, and step by step.
I pick up the pieces, bit by bit.
I put them back together
to be whole again.

Rise! O my soul, from the tears of pity.
Leave the ruins of self-destruction behind.
Find your way through the thorny paths
of life until you reach a peaceful home
where love grows and support flows.

Rise! O my soul beyond the trials
and tribulations of addiction
to drugs and alcohol.
Reach into your inner self.
Open your secret doors
and meet the saving Lord.

The Lord says,
"Child, welcome back.
Now you're home.
I am traveling with you.
I am your light and hope."

Don't panic, O my soul!
Put on the new self and say good-bye
to the old self.

Now I belong to the loving care
of the Lord and AA friends,
who will be saying, "Hi Joe!"

What a feeling! I am not alone!
O my soul! Don't go back
to drugs and alcohol,
but stay with the compassionate Lord,
who will cleanse you from within
and without by the power of His
Holy Spirit
and the wisdom of His word.

The mercy of God, and the loving care
of families and friends have saved me
from addiction and affliction.
Now I am sober, serene, and free.
What a feeling of joy!

Now I enjoy the laughter at home
when my children play with toys,
read books and sing songs.

Now I enjoy the aroma of good food,
the company of a loving wife,
and the association of good friends.

Thank You, O Lord!
You purged my soul with fire and storm.

Now I am in control.
I am happy, sober and grateful
to all the people who helped me.

*(This prayer was written during my attendance
at a course for treating those with
drug or alcohol addictions.)*

How Long, O Lord?

I am always embroiled in trials
and tribulations.
How long
do I have to endure all this
suffering?
O Lord, my God!

Many times,
I have become angry, bitter
and despairing,
but You, O Lord, have chided
me when You said these words to me,
"Child,
why do you not have enough faith in Me?
I want you to know and understand
My purpose in your life."

So I complain, O Lord,
that You may hear me.
I have climbed up the hills,
descended the valleys,
and walked across the plains,
but the pain has been excruciating.

I am anxious, tired and unhappy.
I see no peace in sight,
nor find I any comfort in my life.
I have looked up to the heavens
and begged for help.
I said, "For how long,
O Lord, how long?"

The Lord responded to my plea.
He lifted me up and said,
"Child, you are too important
to Me;
I won't let you fall.
You are Mine.

You are as important as the world
I created,
and as the angels I assigned
to be in charge of your protection.

I would not allow evil
to come near you
nor darkness to overshadow you.
I am your Light and your Savior.

It does not matter how many times
you have denied Me,
nor how many times you turned
your back against Me.
I am here to pick you up,
whenever you stumble and whenever
your burdens are too heavy to carry.

My child, your pain is My pain
and your well-being is My well-being.
I'll always be in your life.
I know that your road is too long
and has many deep pitfalls.

Child, set your eyes on Me
and I will deliver you
from the attacks of the evil forces
of this world."

I said, "O my Lord!
You have seen my needs.
You have known my weaknesses.
Give me strength to face up to my
responsibilities and to carry my Cross
without complaints.
Please help me."

The Lord uplifted my spirit
and, with a gentle voice, said,
"Child, trust Me.

I will save you from pain,
anguish and suffering.
I will give you hope forever
and ever more."

O My God!

Amen, O my God!
You are today with us.
Please enter into our hearts.
Listen to our sighs and prayers.

O my God!
You are with us in space,
at sea and on land.
Enrich our minds, make us aware
of Your presence,
and teach us wisdom.

O my God!
Be merciful and kind to us.
Uplift us with Your compassion
and love.

O my God!
Those who seek the truth will find it
in their hearts;
those who pursue justice
will discover it
in their minds;
and those who struggle
for peace will live it in their souls.

O my God!
We chose our ways over Yours.
You have given us Your covenant,
forgiven us our sins
and provided us with the means
of salvation.
It is up to us to accept You
or turn our back against You.

O my God!
You have been fair, kind and truthful
with us,
but we failed You.
You have granted us to be the masters
of this earth.
We are working very hard to reach
into outer space.

O my God!
The results of our foolishness are
hunger, disease, wars, drugs
and oppression.
All the tears of our hearts
and the cries of our sorrows
are not saving us
from the destruction
of our hands.

O my God!
Those who refuse to know You
will not reap the rewards
of Your forgiveness
and Your salvation.
Those who deny You are destined to
be put away from Your presence.

O my God!
Those who want to have sovereignty
over the affairs of this world cannot
live forever to enjoy their control,
neither here on earth,
nor up there in heaven,
for they chose their way over Yours.

O my God!
Mankind has not done a good job
in running
the affairs of this world.
All that we seek in this world is pain
and more pain, injustice
and more injustice,
prejudice and more prejudice.

Searching

Searching, searching for God
among the poor and the oppressed,
searching for Him
in the hearts and minds
of those who know Him.

Searching, searching for God
among the travelers on land,
in space and at sea,
searching for Him
in the hearts and minds
of those who know Him.

Searching, searching for God
in churches, hospitals, and schools,
searching for Him
in the hearts and minds
of those who know Him.

Searching, searching for God
in work places, parks
and homes,
searching for Him
in the hearts and minds
of those who know Him.

Searching, searching for God
among the disabled, the captives,
and the sick,
searching for Him
in the hearts and minds
of those who know Him.

Searching, searching for God
among the animals of the field,
the birds of the skies
and the fish of the sea,
searching for Him
in the hearts and minds
of those who know Him.

Searching, searching for God
among men, women and children,
searching for Him
in the hearts and minds
of those who know Him.

O my God, *where are You?*
I have been searching for You
since my childhood.

God with a compassionate voice
chided my weary soul,
"Child, search no more,
I have been always with you."

When I heard His voice,
His peace reigned over my heart,
and I now I know that I would be living
in the house of the Lord forever.
Blessed be His name.

I Need A God

I need a God
who will wipe my tears
when I cry.

I need a God
who will call me by my name
when I am alone and lonely.

I need a God
who will remember me
when I am overlooked and forgotten.

I need a God
who will turn evil away from me
when temptation is pursuing me.

I need a God
who will console me
when I feel sad and rejected.

I need a God
who will guide me
when I feel confused
and misguided.

I need a God
who will help me
when I am helpless
and there is no one else
to lift me up.

I need a God
who will tell me about who I am
when I am confused and bewildered.

I need a God
who will take me by the hand
to lift me up
when I am empty and depressed.

I need a God
who will show me the way
when I am lost in the darkness of night.

I need a God
who will empower me
against disease and sickness
when I am weak and frail.

I need a God
who will bring me
to an everlasting peace
and tranquility.

I need a God whose love
will reign in my heart forever.

I found my God in the Lord
Jesus Christ who died for me
on the Cross.

I want Him to love and care for me.
And He will!
Thanks be to Him!

Mother, Pray For Me!

Mother!
Pray for me.
Touch my eyes
with your soft hands
that I may have a peaceful night.

Mother!
Pray for me.
Your prayer will open the doors
of heavens,
and my soul will feel the comfort
of God's love.

My mother lifted her prayer
beyond the stars
and the stars were kindled
like candles
on the altar of God.

I looked upward to the Lord in awe,
and bowed down
before Him to receive His blessings.

The heavenly mist touched my face
and my soul was humbled
by the splendor of His glory.

God's love filled my heart with joy,
and my inner being
sang a song of jubilation.
There are no more pain,
worries and tears.

Mother!
Pray for me.
Pray that the people I meet every day
are kind, helpful and truthful.

Pray for me to live an honest,
just and peaceful life.

My mother's prayers
softened the stings
of my tired soul,
and assured me of a better
outcome in the next world.

Mother!
I ask your forgiveness.
I need your encouragement and support
that I may forgive those who oppress
and persecute me.

Mother!
I am a stranger in this world,
and the tyranny of ignorance
is the enemy of the mind.

Mother!
Calm my fears and ease my worries.
I am tired, disillusioned and angry
with the state of this world.

Mother!
Be there always for me.
Your love is all I need to make it
through the day.

Mother!
Pray for me!

Beatitudes

Blessed are you
when you speak the truth.

Blessed are you
when you defend the truth.

Blessed are you
when you honor the truth,
that you may live an honorable
and peaceful life.

Blessed are you
when you open your heart
in order to receive the "Son of Man."

Blessed are you
when you strive to improve yourself
and you add to the well-being
of mankind.

Blessed are you
when you search for the truth
within your heart, soul and mind.

Blessed are you
when you work hard
in order to spare humanity
from more suffering.

Blessed are you
when you promote prosperity,
peace and good health to all.

Blessed is our God,
the light of our lives,
and the vision of our souls.

Judge Them, O Lord

Lord,
my soul is sad even unto death
when it beholds the people,
who pretend they love You,
defame Your holy name.

They claim that they love You,
but they distort Your truth.
They blaspheme against
Your authority.

They defile Your altar,
ridicule Your authority.
and disdain Your wisdom.

They trade the holiness of Your name
with their greed and arrogance.

They enter Your sanctuary,
but they are strangers to it.

They refuse to listen
to the voice of the Holy Spirit.

Their voices speak loud against You
with obscene and vile language.

Their souls are obsessed
with evil thoughts.
They believe, but their faith
is only in money and vainglory.

They have not accepted You,
nor Your church.

Had they believed in You,
they would have feared Your justice
with humble hearts.

Had they known You,
they would not have stained
themselves
with malice and treachery.

Had they beheld Your glory,
darkness would not have lived
in their hearts.

Had they prayed sincerely
to You,
their viciousness
would not have increased.

Keep their evil away
from Your church,
my God,
and let Your name be holy in
the houses of the saints.

Reserve the purity of Your holy altar
from the touch of the evil ones.

They have dishonored the humble
and the weak.

They have scorned the poor
and the lame.

They have blasphemed, O Lord!
Judge them
according to their evil deeds.

They have lifted the pillars
of their homes
to make them dens of iniquity.
They made Your house a center
of darkness,
and abuse the people
who truly believe in You.

They have not known You
in their hearts.
They have deserted You
in order to live in the darkness
of their souls.

Judge their iniquities, O Lord!
Vindicate the innocent
and protect them
from oppression.

Protect the poor
from the tyranny of the rich.

Save the saints from the power
of the unjust.

Let Your name be holy
on the lips of the believers.

Let Your name be holy
in the hearts of the forgotten
and the oppressed.
Let Your right hand
crush your enemies.

Be a protector and a guide
to the poor,
the weak, and the sick.

O Lord, let the unbelievers repent.
Let them turn away
from evil that they may
know You,
and live virtuous lives.

I Am Not Alone

No, I am not alone!
No, I am not alone!
The Lord is with me.
I am not alone!
The Lord is with me.

He is with me.
He is with you and me.

He is my Companion
and Counselor.
He is with you and me.

I am no longer depressed
and in despair.
The Lord is with you and me.

I am joyful and happy;
the Lord is with me.
He is with you and me.

I have a friend in you,
my brother and sister.
The Lord is with you and me.
The Lord is with you and me.
He answers my prayers.

I am at peace with myself.
The Lord is with you and me.

O you people of the earth,
allow the Lord
to enter into your hearts.
The Lord is with you and me.

The Lord Jesus is knocking
on your door and mine.
O Lord Jesus!
Please come into my heart.

I am no longer crying
nor grieving.
The bells are ringing;
the joy of the Lord
is with you and me.

I am no longer down and out.
I am happy.
The Lord is with you and me.
O people of the earth!
Rejoice!
The Lord is with you and me.

Please, O my Lord,
come into my heart.
I am no more lonely
and depressed.
The Lord is with you and me.

Walk To The Crucifix

Today is the day,
you and I
must work together
for the better,
but it can't be done
unless we become brothers.

If you and I are supposed
to be equal,
why then must I hunger
while you gloat in silver?

It is not fair that I must ail
and suffer,
while you hold the key
to the medicine.

Before you pass any judgment,
walk with me to the Crucifix;
what do you see,
forgiveness or anger?

You hold many keys;
why don't you open the doors
to allow in tired feet?

Let us celebrate
a joyful feast,
where the privileged
and the beggar chat and eat.

Let there be no more need,
nor anyone be full of greed,
but
all become happy indeed!

Be My Friend, O My Lord!

My God and Lord!
When I meet new people,
I feel uneasiness, apprehension
and anxiety.
Please help me to understand them
that I may be their friend.

When I feel lonely and scared,
be with me, O my Lord,
and give me
the confidence and the courage I need
to be in control of my life.

Oftentimes,
I feel loneliness and isolation creeping
into my heart,
and I become frightened and confused.

I have no support and no friends.
Be my friend.
Help me to make friends.

Provide me with the wisdom,
the confidence and the patience
to interact with people
with honesty, openness
and friendliness.

Guide me to meet the right people.
Help me to learn
about what I don't know.

Give me the wisdom to be kind,
honest and fair.

I pray that You may strengthen
my trust in You and in my family
with the support
I receive from You and them.

Please don't allow temptations
to undermine my belief in You
nor to weaken my resolve
to achieve my goals.

Be with me always,
guard me with Your holy angels,
day and night.

I pray that I may not go astray from
Your sovereign authority.
Please don't allow evil
to have power over me.

All I want is to be genuine, trustworthy,
and faithful, and to be kind to others
without prejudgment or criticism.
All I want is to be a decent friend
and a productive citizen.

I would like to be loyal to You
and the people who love You.
Help me to be a team player.
Protect me from the pleasures of the flesh.
In Your name, Lord Jesus, I pray, Amen.

So I Dream On!

I dream a lot of dreams;
only a few of them come true,
but it is enough for me
to keep on dreaming.

I pray many prayers;
the Lord answers
only a few of them,
but it is enough for me
to keep on praying.

I trust many friends;
many of them turn against me,
but a few stay with me,
and that is enough for me
to continue on trusting.

I sow many seeds in the soil;
the insects eat many of them,
but enough of them grow for me.
So I keep on sowing.

I have been put down
many times,
and many days pass by
without a smile,
but there are enough smiles
for me
to keep on smiling.

I help many people;
many of them abuse
my kindness,
but a few of them appreciate
what I do for them.
So I continue on helping.

I make many decisions.
I don't know
whether what I am doing is right,
but I have enough faith
in my God.
So I continue on making them.

I Will Go On My Journey

When hope leaves you,
despair will visit you;
and when life appears
to be worthless,
a new spirit
will sprout in your soul.

When the road is full of pitfalls,
the light turns into darkness,
and the dangers multiply,
a voice from within calls on you
not to cancel your journey.

When anguish is intense,
anxiety overwhelming,
and the heart is weary,
a new energy surges
in your body
not to forsake your journey.

When life is full of misery,
the conscience of guilt,
and the mind of confusion,
a light appears to you at the end
of the tunnel
to guide your journey.

When letdowns crush your spirit,
frustrations your heart,
and failures your pride,
this is the time you need
to continue with your journey.

When you are at the end
of your rope,
hanging by a thread,
and it is so dark around you,
this is the time
the Lord will lift you up
and wipe away your tears.

(You may replace the word "journey"
with the word "decision,"
and you will have a new poem
with a new meaning.)

Listen To Me, O My Lord!

O God, my God!
Once I said to those who say
to me,
"How do you feel?"
"Don't ask me,
'How do you feel?'
unless you are
willing to listen to me!"

We often say,
"How do you feel?"
But we don't mean it,
nor are we willing to listen
to each other with empathy.
But, You, O Lord, are the One
who listens and cares
for my well-being.

You are the One who knows
the inner heart
with Your infinite knowledge,
and touches our lives with Your love
and compassion.
You are the One who calls us
into Your service
in order to complete
Your mission in our lives.

You consecrate us
to be the instruments
of Your peace in the world.

O Lord, my God!
I cannot hide my face
from Your presence,
nor can I keep my complaints away
from You,
especially when our daily affairs
are rough and tough.

Every day, I see the complexity
of our lives
and the ambiguity
of our difficult decisions.

It does not matter how hard
we plan our worldly affairs,
we always face new problems
and new challenges.
No one can help us, but You,
O Lord!
Whether we think out loud or quietly,
our integrity is what counts the most,
and our genuine honesty
is what we need in order to combat evil.

Help us to accept whom we really are,
and teach us to be tolerant and helpful
to one another.

O God, my God!
Your way is the way,
and our way is vainglory.

Dwell in our hearts and deliver
us from evil.
Make us worthy of Your love.

My heart calls on You.
My mind is overwhelmed
by Your presence,
and life is the creation
of Your infinite wisdom.

O Lord, my God!
You are the one who soothes our pain,
heals our suffering,
and gives us hope of a better world.

O Lord, my God!
I feel Your love and compassion.

Help us in order to overcome the pain
of our short comings.
Guide us to listen to ourselves
and each other.

O Lord, my God!
Listen to us and help us to cope
with our weaknesses.

Cleanse our hearts from pride,
arrogance and self-pity.
Please listen to my plea, Lord,
that I may listen to You.

I know that You are in my heart,
mind and soul.
Give me strength to keep You
in my life.

God Of Life

God of life!
Protect me
and have mercy
on my wounded heart.

I am calling on You
at break of dawn;
don't ignore me,
nor turn Your face away from me.
I am calling on You in the evening;
don't forget me during the night.

I am opening my heart to You;
don't turn Your face away from me.
I am weak and unhappy,
I am in need of You
to help me find my way
in the world of the living.

God of life!
My heart is bleeding.
My spirit is broken.
I feel hurt.
Help me.
Heal my wounds

I pray for those who no longer
preach forgiveness,
reconciliation and redemption.
Please hear my prayer.

God of life!
Many people groan and moan;
they are insensitive
to the needs of others,
but You are always sensitive
to our needs.
Come, dwell in us, and help us.

I walk among many people,
and I feel like a stranger among them.
Be my friend and counselor.
I have been speaking
to the people of God,
but they claim
that their way is the way.

Help me to be kind and helpful
to others,
even to those who abused
my kindness.

God of life!
I feel as if I have become a victim
of indifference.
Bless my heart and save me
from the snares of the enemy.

I pass by many people
and greet them,
but they stare at me
as if I were an alien.

I look into the heavens
to seek wisdom and guidance
that I may make it through the day.
But every day gets harder.

Woe is me in this trivial world!

God of life!
You are the dwelling place of my soul.
Listen to my pleas and prayers.
Grant me peace and harmony,
O my Lord.

God of life!
The world is blind
to Your tolerance
and kindness.

Please grant me the ability
to understand
that we all need to work
for eternal peace.

Amen, O My Lord!

Amen when we speak with You
and when You listen to us.

Amen when we speak out
against hatred and evil,
and when You provide us
with harmony and stability.

Amen when we seek kindness
and love to soften the blows
and soothe the pain,
and when You bless us with
Your grace.

Amen when we are fair and tolerant
of one another
and when we improve the quality
of life.

Amen when we forgive
one another and make up
for what we did wrong,
and when You show us the way.

Amen when we pray for
compassion and mercy
to reconcile ourselves with You,
and when You open the door
for us to be with You.

Amen when we reject violence
and promote peace,
and when You teach us
to be the disciples of peace.

Amen when we upgrade
each other's skills
to increase in efficiency,
and when You teach us
competency and proficiency.

Amen when we accept each other
for what we are
to get rid of bigotry and prejudice,
and when You admonish us
to love one another.

Amen when we communicate,
with one another to understand
and understand to communicate,
and when You communicate
with us the word of Your truth.

Amen for being a good God
who saves our souls from destruction.

In Your name, Lord Jesus, I pray,
Amen.

Bless The Lord, O My Soul!

Bless the Lord, O my soul.
Blessed is He for restoring me
with His compassion, forgiveness
and grace.

Bless the Lord, O my soul.
Blessed is He for delivering me
from the jaws of poverty,
the evil thoughts of the day
and the horrible dreams of the night.

Bless the Lord, O my soul.
Blessed is He for giving me life
and for filling me with the grace
of the Holy Spirit.

Bless the Lord, O my soul.
Blessed is He for restoring me
and for showing me the way
to live in His house forever.

Bless the Lord, O my soul.
Blessed is He for restoring my
honor and dignity
and for making my life
a shining light for all the people.

Bless the Lord, O my soul.
Blessed is He for healing me
from sickness and disease
and for keeping my life safe
from the assaults of the dark forces.

Bless the Lord, O my soul.
Blessed is He for sparing me
from the pain of hunger
and from the wants of poverty.

Bless the Lord, O my soul.
Blessed is He for loving and caring for me.

Bless the Lord, O my soul.
Blessed is He for knowing
the secrets of my heart
and for the understanding
of my probing mind.

Bless the Lord, O my soul.
Blessed is He for correcting my ways,
for healing my wounds
and for giving me life everlasting
for His name's sake.

Bless the Lord, O my soul.
Blessed is He
for making me as white as snow
and for filling me
with His love, peace, and joy.

Bless the Lord, O my soul.
Blessed is He for accepting me
among the chosen ones
and for granting me
the gift of redemption and salvation.

Bless the Lord, O my soul.
Blessed is He for restoring me
in order to live in His house forever.

The Lord Is In My Heart

The Lord
is within my heart,
I knew it then,
and I know it now.

I will not waiver,
nor will I cry,
for the Lord
is in my heart.

I will not retreat,
nor will I hide,
for the Lord lives in my heart.

I will not have fear,
nor will I scream,
for the Lord lives in my heart.

I will dream dreams,
and pray prayers,
for the Lord
is in my heart.

I Asked

I asked for patience,
but I was told *to wait.*

I asked for help,
but I was told I am *on my own.*

I asked for support to control my anger,
but I was told this is my problem,
and I need to deal with it *alone.*

I asked for clarity of thought,
but the more I asked,
the more *I became confused.*

I asked for good health and well-being,
but I entertained pain *all day long.*

I asked You for riches and comfort,
but I was given the choice to struggle
for my daily bread.

I asked for safety and security,
but I felt unsafe and insecure
in *an ungodly world.*

I asked for a status and influence,
but I was given a shield
and armor.

I asked for wisdom and vision,
but I was taught simplicity
and humility in what *I say and do.*

I became very impatient.
I said,
"Lord, when will You respond
to my pleas?"

The Lord answered,
"All you need is My grace."

The Lord Always Surprises Me

Whenever I reach a dead end
and I can't go any further,
the Lord steps in
to build a new bridge for me
to go further and further
until I reach my destiny.

Whenever I reach a cliff
and am ready to fall down,
the Lord steps in
and transports me into safety.

Whenever I feel tired
and can't go any further,
the Lord breathes energy
into my life
and gives me a new beginning.

Whenever I become unable
to serve myself and others,
the Lord taps me on the back
and says,
"Child, your job is not finished."
All of a sudden, a rush of energy
pervades my whole being.
So I hurry to finish all my errands.

Whenever I feel sad and depressed,
the Lord comes to me and says,
"Child,
you have so many things to do,
you're not going to be sad
and depressed."
Suddenly
I begin to feel more joyful,
going about tending to my business.

Whenever I can do no more
and am at the end of my rope,
the Lord always steps in to save me.

So, I know the Lord always
surprises me.

Hold Me To Your Post

Hold me to your post,
O Lord,
to Your post, hold me.

When my world is falling apart,
and failures are shaking my heart,
I break apart.

Please come into my heart,
and hold me to Your post,
O Lord,
to Your post, hold me.

When my tears
are running like a flood,
and my soul is trembling
from trouble;
I feel despondent with hopelessness.
So I cry, Lord,
come and help me.
I need You.

Hold me to your post,
O Lord,
to Your post, hold me.

When I am overwhelmed
with confusion,
and my mind is impaired
with illusion,
I become helpless in seclusion.

So I cry, Lord,
please come to my help,
I need You
to hold me to Your post,
to Your post, hold me.

Where Are You?

Lord!
"Where are you?"
You keep asking me.

Whether I belong to You,
or to the world,
You are my Lord.

You are my Savior.
Please, come and save me.

Hear me, O Lord!
Extend Your hands,
and lift me up.

Lord! *"Where are you?"*
You keep asking me.

Whether I am happy,
or full of misery,
You know all about me,
O my God.

Lord!
I'm standing here before You.
Come and save a wretch like me.

Lord!
You keep asking,
"Where are you?"
"Do you love Me?"
You know where I am,
and that I love You.

Can You hear me,
Are You listening to me?

Lord!
Why do You keep asking me,
"Where are you?"

You know all about me,
whether I am lost or found.
Please, come and save me
that I may always be with You.

I am nothing without You.
Please come
and dwell in my heart.

I Rejoice In The Lord

I rejoice in the Lord when He saves me
from harm and danger,
and when He commands me
to respect His authority.

I rejoice in Him when He corrects my ways
and when He teaches me
to follow His directions.

I rejoice in Him when He guides me
through the hardships of life
and uplifts my spirit
when I am discouraged.

I rejoice in Him when He is with me
and when He spares my life
from the blindness
of the noonday
and the terror of night.

I rejoice in Him when He sets
my feet aright
and cleanses my heart
from anger and hate.

I rejoice in Him
when He gives me a clean tongue
and when He fills me
with the wisdom of His words.

I rejoice in Him when He walks with me
through the darkness of night
and when He stands by me
when I fall down.

I rejoice in Him when He extends me
the grace of forgiveness
and the gift of redemption
and salvation.

I rejoice in the Lord for He turns
my defeat into victory
and my setbacks into triumph.

I rejoice in the Lord when he turns
the impossible odds
into possible opportunities
and when He grants me victory.

I rejoice in Him
when He restores my soul
and when He makes me
as white as snow.

I rejoice in Him
when He calls me *'My child'*
and when I call Him *'My Father.'*

I rejoice in Him for allowing me
to live in His house forever.

I Am Glad You're My Dad!

Dad is a wonderful man.
His love touches my heart.

He soothes my pain
with the drops of his tears,
and comforts me
with the joy of his smiles.

He wakes me up in the morning
to go to school,
and tucks me in bed at night.

I feel safe whenever I have a bad fall,
for he is always there for me.

Dad charms me with his wit,
and reads me a variety of books.

He helps me with my homework.
We play together,
and have all kinds of fun.

Dad is my hero and superman.
I kiss him, hang around his neck,
and give him a bear hug.
His hand holds mine.
I feel warm and happy
whenever he is around.

I enjoy calling him,
"Daddy!"
I love to hear him calling me,
"Child!"

How beautiful it is
when we both watch
the rising sun,
look for the stars at night,
and reflect on the moon on the horizon.

Daddy buys me clothes, toys,
books, and games.

I love Daddy.
I want to be like him.
He is a loving and caring man.

Daddy takes me to picnics
and restaurants.
He keeps watch over me
even when I am gone.

I love Daddy.
I want to be wise like him.

Every day
I weigh and measure myself.
I want to be just like him.

Dad!
I love what you do for me.
Aren't you glad
I am your child?

No Education Without You,
O My Lord

Educate us to sow the word of truth
among the children.

Dedicate our minds to know the truth.

Uplift our spirits to kindle our hopes.

Care for our needs
that we may not fall into despair.

Arm us with love and compassion
to care for the poor and the needy.

Teach us to be educators
and scholars for all generations.

Inspire us to work with diligence
and determination
in order to eliminate hunger
and oppression.

O Lord! How great are Your wonders?

No one can doubt the greatness
of Your power and glory.

May Your blessings uplift us
with Your inspiration
to learn and teach in Your name, Amen!

This Is Their Glory

We watch our children grow,
today and tomorrow.

We watch them grasp and grope,
study and learn,
love and care,
earn and prosper
in a world of their own.

We watch them wonder,
search and explore through their garden
of intrigue until they reach their goals.

They are our future.
They are our world --
not yet men and women,
but boys and girls
who march forward, turning keys
until they open the right doors.

Their eyes glow like the stars in the skies,
with new visions and clear hopes.

Their youth and their minds
are as precious as pearls and gold.

This is their time!
This is their glory!

They will treasure their achievements
in their life-long story.

Our children are gentle and strong,
ambitious and determined
to continue on.

This is their beginning
as they look for a world beyond.

They look for a loving God
to welcome them into His fold.

May their years be many,
and full of joy.
May their lives be full of love,
and the peace of the Lord.

All in Your name, Lord Jesus,
Amen.

Who Taught Us?

Who taught the birds to fly
and the trees upward to grow?

Who ordered the river to flow
and the ocean waves to roar?

Who told the sun
on the horizon to rise
and the earth to bring forth food?

Who advised the mind
to create thoughts
and the heart to pump out blood?

Who informed the galaxies
to hang in space
and life to sustain our souls?

Who inspired the writer to write
and the musician to play music?

Who supplied us with the air
to breathe,
and instructed the children
to be born?

Who directed the earth
to go round and round
and the stars in the skies to shine?

Who instructed the builders
to build schools
and students to attain their goals?

Who created man and woman
into the world
to procreate life
and be the masters of the earth?

You created them all, O Lord,
glory be to You!

Salute To Our Nation

We, the people,
are proud of our nation.

We, with the beat of the drums,
the rumble of guns,
and the music of hymns,
salute our Colors.

We rise with the sun,
toil the land,
and sweat in the mines.

Our ships sail the seas,
our soldiers keep the peace,
and our citizens preach brotherhood.

Year after year,
we get stronger, bolder and better.
We safeguard the freedom of expression.

We are always ready and prepared,
to repel the attacks of all the enemies.

Our freedom is sacred
in this beloved land.

Our security and peace are where
we always take a stand.

Wherever our soldiers dig in at foothills,
stand on mountain tops,
or fold the plains under their feet,
they ring the bells of liberty,
justice and brotherhood
in the four corners of the earth.

We preach tolerance, live in freedom,
and fight with courage.
We are the students of history.

We accept responsibility,
silence hostility and encourage harmony
among all the peoples.

We are masters of the seas,
lords of the mountains,
and hawks of the skies.

The seas know our gallantry,
the hills our bravery,
and the skies our victories.
Salute our nation!

The Proud Sailor

There is always a Sailor
who lies at the bottom of the sea
and, at one time,
he defended his country.

There is always a Sailor
who wears the uniform
and still carries the spirit
of patriotism in his heart.

There is always a Sailor who
stands tall to salute the Colors
with ecstasy and pride.

There is always a Sailor
who is prepared and ready
to defend his homeland.

There is always a Sailor
who is ready to protect
liberty and justice for all.

There is always a Sailor
who promotes progress
to keep his country
ahead of all other countries
in spirituality, science, and
technology.

There is always a Sailor
who upholds spiritual, moral
and social values.

There is always a Sailor
who keeps God as his
Champion in peace and war.

Let us honor all sailors
with honor and dignity
for their sacrifices
and contributions
to our nation.

In Your name, Lord Jesus, I pray,
Amen.

Thanksgiving

Thank You, Lord,
for Your gifts and blessings on all of us.

Heal our infirmities
that we may always appreciate
Your loving care.

Assure us
of Your continuous love
and protection
that we may live in peace.

Never leave us
alone without Your guidance
and support
that we may be called,
"the children of God."

Kindle our faith
with inspiration and motivation
and the will to succeed.

Save us
from our foolishness and indifference
that we may become the heirs
of Your kingdom.

Give us wisdom
that we may make the right decisions
and that we may not stumble
in the darkness of ignorance.

Inspire us
to be enlightened
with Your wisdom and understanding
that we may care for one another.

Visit us
when we are helpless
and sick,
and when we are hurt and in pain.

Intensify our desire
to seek improvement in our lives
that we may take care for our families.

Name us
among the chosen ones
that we may give our full measure
to serve You.

Grant us
to be forgiving, caring and loving.

We Give You Thanks

We thank the Lord our God
for all that we have.

We thank Him
when we see the light of the day,
and enjoy the stillness of night.

We thank Him when we take a walk,
meet a neighbor or greet a friend.

We thank Him
when we watch our children grow,
and share our love and kindness
with them.

We thank Him
when we gaze into the heavens
to ponder the depth
of His infinite wisdom.

We thank Him for the air we breathe,
the water we drink,
and the clothes we wear.

We thank Him for the labor
of our hands
and the fruits of the land.
He provides food for the hungry
and hope for the broken-hearted.

The Lord is the light of our lives
and the source of our strength.

He furnishes us with comfort
and hope.

He protects us
from the pitfalls of our ignorance.

How beautiful it is to watch
all the living enjoy the freedom
of life,
bathe in the running streams
of living water,
and quench their thirst.

Let us reflect and examine
our hearts and minds.

Let us pledge our loyalty to Him.
Let us give support, tolerance
and understanding to one another
with honesty, love, and forgiveness.

May the spirit of the loving God
provide us with the opportunity
to enjoy life with all its
blessings.

In Your name, Lord Jesus, I pray,
Amen.

Embrace Me, O My Lord!

To You I lift up my prayers,
O my Lord.
Lift me up from my pain.
I beg You, Lord Jesus,
please help me.

To You I lift up my pleas,
hear my voice.
Give me Your peace,
O my Savior.

To You I lift up all my pain,
and ask for Your compassion.
Hear my cries!

Embrace me with Your love,
and allow me to thank You
for Your kindness.

Open for me the doors
of Your mercy,
O my Lord,
and grant me the right
to receive Your comfort and peace.

In Your name, Lord Jesus,
I pray, Amen.

Come To Your Rest

In Your arms,
hold me in Your arms,
O my Lord;
hold me in Your arms.

In Your arms, please hold me.

My spirit is lifted up to You,
to You my spirit is lifted;
hold me in Your arms.

Allow me to hear Your words,
"Child, you are in My arms,
please come home with Me;
you've done well.

Please come with Me,
I have a special place for you.
You're dear to Me.
Please come in with Me,
you're dear to Me.
Please come in,
I have a place for you.

Come in to My comfort and joy.
Come in and have peace;
have eternal peace.

Come with Me;
I am holding you in my arms.
You are in My arms.

Now You are home.
My home is your home.
Please come into your eternal rest.
Come to your eternal peace."

Eternal rest is granted to you.
Now you may rest in peace!

In Jesus' name I pray,
Amen.

I Have Seen Your Light

I have seen Your light
coming down
from heaven,
O Lord!

It has transformed me
into a being of light.

I feel Your peace in my heart,
it is bliss from within.

I hear Your voice
calling me by name,
"Child, it's time
for your eternal peace.

Rest your head
over My breast,
and wrap your hands
around Mine.

Lean on Me,
let Me carry you
the rest of the way.

Your soul is a part of Mine,
and Mine is a part of yours.

Have peace!
My peace is your peace!
Rest in peace."

The Lord Is My Shepherd

The Lord is my shepherd
and the shield of my life.

He is my protector in time of stress
and need.

He delivers me from the pitfalls
of my foolishness and,
in the darkness of night,
He guides me with His light into safety.

He keeps my head up high with honor,
and saves my soul
from the anguish of hard times.

He provides me with food and shelter,
and shields me from the dangers
of the assaults of evil.

He welcomes me to His home
where I find family and friends.

He provides me with comfort and joy.
I enjoy His presence because
He is gentle and kind to my heart.

He safeguards my life,
and readily answers my prayer
when I am in need or in pain.

My soul praises the Lord
who corrects my ways,
washes my sins and makes me
as white as snow.

Blessed is the Lord who sanctifies
my soul,
and purifies my heart and mind.

Blessed is the Lord my God
who loves and cares for me,
for He is all good.

Blessed is He by all His angels,
and all those who love the beauty
of His house.

Blessed is the Lord
who grants me all the honors,
and the privileges of His blessings.
Blessed is He who redeems,
and saves my soul
in order to live
in His house forever.

In Jesus' name I pray,
Amen.

Memory Eternal

O Lord, our God,
at these moments of remembrance,
lift our hearts and thoughts beyond
the darkness of death to the light
of Your presence.

We pray that You may receive Your
child *(Name)* who departed this life
into Your world of comfort and peace.

Your servant *(Name)* left our world to reside
with Your saints who
accepted the faith and believed
in Your call to salvation and everlasting life.

We pray that You may recruit him/her among
the children of light with Your saints
and the holy angels who obey Your will
and carry out Your command.

Your servant *(Name)* left this world,
its struggles, fears and anxieties,
and now he/she resides in Your mansion
where there is no more pain,
sorrow and tears.

O Lord, our God, at this time,
we ask You to forgive his/her sins whether
voluntary or involuntary,
whether by thought, word or deed.

Bestow Your blessings and comfort upon his/
her family, relatives and friends,
who are here to bid him/her
farewell, and to pray for the rest of his/her soul.

We pray that his/her pleasant memories
will sustain all of them with consolation,
understanding and peace.

We pray that You will comfort them
during this time of grief, pain and sorrow.

We pray that the departure of *(Name)*
from this world
would fill our minds with gentle thoughts
and pleasant memories.

Lord God!
You assured us
with Your forgiveness,
redemption and salvation.

You assured us of Your faithfulness to us.
We pray that we are faithful to You.

Now we know that he/she is free from
fear of death
because he/she found refuge in You.

Guide us to be loyal to You
and to cherish his/her memories
with kindness and respect.

Eternal rest grant unto him/her, O Lord,
that Your light may always shine on him/
her forever and ever more.

In Your name, Lord Jesus, I pray,
Amen.

Memory eternal! (3 times)

Farewell

We bid you farewell.
We say, "Good-bye to you!"

In sadness and joy,
we shared many memories.

We felt the touch of your heart,
and the warmth of your spirit.

The time we knew each other
was pleasant,
and the memories were precious.

Across the land and under the sun,
we carry in our hearts
the love you shared
and the care you exemplified.

Good-bye, my friend!
Fair wind and smooth sailing
to the end of your journey.
So long to you!

May the face of Almighty God
touch you as you touched us
with your cheerful face
and kind smiles.

May we meet again
when we assemble in
God's kingdom
to share the fruits of His victory.

Bon voyage!
Godspeed!

May His blessings accompany you
and your family
to the end of your journey.

All in Jesus' name,
Amen.

About the author:

Background

The Reverend John A. Shalhoub is the son of Andraos Ferris Shalhoub and Nour Yousef Habib. He was born in Aita El-Foukhar, Lebanon, February 25, 1943. He studied for the Ministry in the Balamand Seminary from 1958 to 1964. He was transferred to the Antiochian Orthodox Patriarchate in Damascus, Syria and worked in the Assyia Schools from 1964 to 1966.

The Reverend John Andraos Shalhoub came to the United States on November 5, 1966 at the request of Archbishop Michael Shaheen at the urging of his Uncle George Ferris Shalhoup of Charleston, West Virginia. He enrolled in the University of Toledo, Ohio majoring in psychology from 1966 to 1968.

Archbishop Michael Shaheen ordained the Reverend John Shalhoub as an Antiochian Orthodox Priest on February 23, 1969 at St. George Orthodox Church of South Glens Falls, New York and he served there from 1969 to 1975. He then served at St. Catherine Orthodox Church of Glens Falls, New York from 1975 to 1982.

The Reverend John Andraos Shalhoub was commissioned as an Eastern Orthodox Navy Chaplain, on March 19, 1982 with the rank of Lieutenant and was promoted to Lieutenant Commander on April 1, 1986.

Since 1985, the Reverend John Andraos Shalhoub has held the positions of teacher, counselor, and Enrichment Educator in the Onslow County School System, Jacksonville, North Carolina. He was an instructor of Psychology and Sociology at Coastal Community College of Jacksonville, N. C. from 1986 to 1992. His writings on educational, family and spiritual issues appear periodically in the *Daily News* of Jacksonville, North Carolina. The Reverend John A. Shalhoub has his own practice, *Shalhoub Family Counseling Services,* since 1990. He provides psychotherapy, family counseling and school counseling.

Education
Religious Education:
* Balamand Seminary, Ministerial Education and Training, El-Koura, Tripoli, Lebanon, 1964

Undergraduate:
* Toledo University, Toledo, Ohio, Social Science, 1968
* Adirondack Community College, Glens Falls, New York, English and Social Science, 1969
* Siena College, Loudonville, New York, Sociology, 1970

Graduate Studies:
* St. Rose College, Albany, New York, Educational Psychology, 1972
* Plattsburgh University College, Psychology, 1971
* Fuller Theological Seminary, Pasadena, California, Doctor of Ministry, 1984
* East Carolina University, Greenville, North Carolina School and Clinical Counseling, 1992

Licensed And Certified
* Guidance Counselor, East Carolina University, Department of Public Instruction, Greenville, North Carolina, 1992
* English and Social Studies Teacher, 7-12, Albany, New York, 1977
* An ordained Orthodox Priest, Antiochian Christian Orthodox Archdiocese, Toledo, Ohio, 1969
* An Eastern Orthodox Chaplain, United States Navy, 1982
* National Certified Counselor, Greensboro, North Carolina, 1990

- Licensed Practicing Counselor, Raleigh, North Carolina, 1990
- A member of the American Counseling Association, 1990
- A member of the National Education Association, 1985
- A member of the North Carolina Association of educators, 1985
- A member of the Antiochian Orthodox Christian archdiocese, 1966
- North Carolina Advancement of Teaching seminars, 1991 and 1993

Family

The Reverend John A. Shalhoub is married to Awatif Mitri Ghareeb and the Lord blessed them with three boys-- George Joseph, Michael Paul and Samuel David. He has three brothers: George, Elias and Joseph and two sisters: Rose and Mary.

Acknowledgement

I am grateful for my Antiochian Christian heritage. "And the apostles were called Christians first in Antioch." (ACTS 11:26), KJV.

We live for today. We live our lives for today, and we hope what is good for today is good for tomorrow, but the uncertainty of tomorrow inspires our today's faith and hope for a peaceful and everlasting life. Lord, even when we give up on You, You won't give up on us!

* * * * *

I am grateful to my God and Lord Jesus Christ and all the people who helped and inspired me in this world to stay on course to achieve my goals. Also, I am grateful for the encouragement of my family: My mother Nour, my sister Rose, and my cousin Judy Shalhoup. At this time I would like to remember my sister Mary Shalhoub and my cousin Carolyn Shalhoup who are no longer with us in this world.

I pray for the thrice-blessed Patriarch Theodosius Abou-Rejayli, and the thrice-blessed Archbishop Michael Shaheen who are no longer with us. I pray for his Beatitude, the Patriarch Ignatius Hazim, Metropolitan Archbishop, Philip Saliba, his Grace Bishop Elias Najm, and his Grace Bishop Demetri Khoury for making a difference in my life. Also I am grateful *to members of St. George Orthodox Church of South Glens Falls, New York and to the members of St. Catherine Orthodox Church of Glens Falls, New York,* for their support while I was their pastor. May the Lord our God reside in our hearts and minds in order to do His will, and to carry on with His mission.

"The stone which the builders refused is become the head stone of the corner" (Psalm 118:22), KJV.

The Reverend John A. Shalhoub

207